THE
INCAS

TIM WOOD

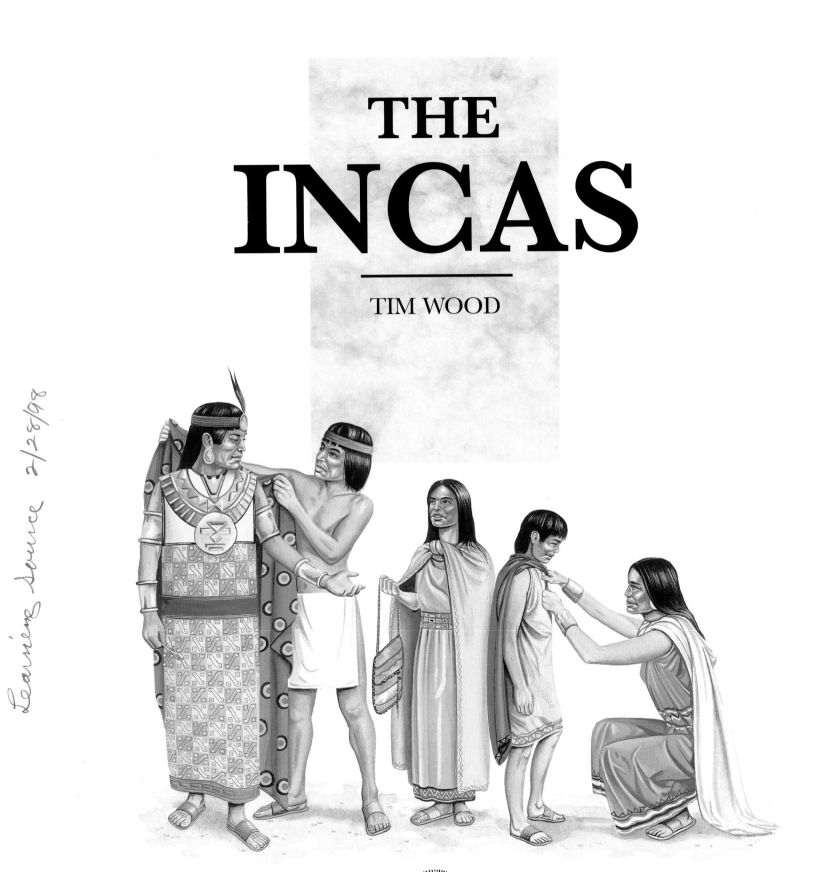

Viking

Acknowledgments

The publishers would like to thank Bill Le Fever, who illustrated the see-through pages;
James Field, who illustrated the cover; and the organizations that have given their
permission to reproduce the following pictures:

American Museum of Natural History/Courtesy Department Library Services Tr.5004(2)/
Photo by John Bigelow Taylor: 44 above right.
Ancient Art and Architecture Collection: 29 below right, 30 above left, 34 above left, 35 above right.
Bildarchiv Preussischer Kulturbesitz/Staatliche Museen zu Berlin—Museum für Volkekunde: 12 below left.
Bridgeman Art Library/British Museum, London: 44 below right, /Gilray 45 above right.
The Art Institute of Chicago: Photograph copyright 1994. All Rights Reserved. South America, North Coast Peru,
Lambeyeque Valley, Chimu-Inca style, Ritual vessel representing woman with an aryballos, ceramic c.1480,
23.8 x 18.4 cm Buckingham Fund 1955.2411. Photograph by Robert Hashimoto: 31 above right.
E.T. Archive/National Museum Archaeology, Lima: 27 above right.
Werner Forman Archive/Museum für Volkekunde, Berlin: 12 above left, 17 above right,
26 below left, 26 above right, 29 above center, 45 below left.
Photographie Giraudon: 18 above left, 19 above right.
Robert Harding Picture Library: 15 above right, /Amano Museum, Lima 26 above left, /
Robert Frerck 28 above left, /Christopher Rennie 18 above right.
Michael Holford: 4 above left, 5 below right, 7 below right.
Magnum Photos/Stuart Franklin: 9 above right, 36 above center left, 36 above left.
MAS: 42 above left. **South American Pictures:** 6 above left, 23 below right, 37 below right,
43 above right, /Tony Morrison 11 above right, 21 below right, 29 above right, 35 below right.
The Textile Museum, Washington, D.C./91.395: 29 above left.

Illustrators
Peter Bull: 5, 14 top left. **James Field (Simon Girling):** cover. **Ray Grinaway:** title page, 4, 8, 9 bottom right, 10, 10-11, 20, 21, 28.
Christian Hook: 14, 15, 18, 19, 26-27. **Richard Hook (Linden Artists):** 46-47. **Bill Le Fever:** 16-17, 24-25, 32-33, 40-41.
Tony Randall: 22, 23 (both), 30, 31, 44. **Mark Stacey:** 6-7, 7, 9 top right, 12, 13, 38-39, 39, 42, 43. **Simon Williams:** 34, 35, 36-37, 37.

VIKING
Published by the Penguin Group
Penguin Books USA Inc., 375 Hudson Street, New York, New York 10014, U.S.A.
Penguin Books Ltd, 27 Wrights Lane, London W8 5TZ, England
Penguin Books Australia Ltd, Ringwood, Victoria, Australia
Penguin Books Canada Ltd, 10 Alcorn Avenue, Toronto, Ontario, Canada M4V 3B2
Penguin Books (N.Z.) Ltd, 182–190 Wairau Road, Auckland 10, New Zealand

Penguin Books Ltd, Registered Offices: Harmondsworth, Middlesex, England

First published in Great Britain by Heinemann Children's Reference,
a division of Reed Educational and Professional Publishing Ltd., 1996
First published in the United States of America by Viking,
a division of Penguin Books USA Inc., 1996

1 3 5 7 9 10 8 6 4 2

Copyright © Reed Educational and Professional Publishing Ltd., 1996

Library of Congress Catalog Card Number: 96 — 60285

ISBN 0-670-87037-4

Printed in Belgium

CONTENTS

Origins of the Incas 4
The Empire 6
The Inca People 8
The Sapa Inca 10
The Government 12
Cuzco—the Capital City 14
Palace on the Lake 16
Engineering the Land 18
Food and Farming 20
The Role of Women 22
Houses and Homes 24
Arts and Crafts 26
Clothes and Fashion 28
Growing Up 30
Temples of the Sun 32
Priests and Doctors 34
The Army 36
Travel and Trade 38
Messengers 40
The Spanish Arrive 42
Conquest of the Empire 44
Key Dates and Glossary 46
Index 48

The Incas learned gold working skills from peoples they conquered, like the Chimus. This 12th–13th century Chimu vase is made of gold and decorated with turquoise.

About 50,000 years ago, the first people came to North America across a land bridge that joined northeast Asia to present day Alaska. By about 10,000 B.C. their descendants had spread into South America. Some became hunter-gatherers in the lush Amazonian rain forest. Others became farmers in what is now Peru. It was from this group, about 6,000 years ago, that the first significant South American civilizations began to emerge.

A HARD LAND

The western side of South America is a harsh, mountainous region dominated by the craggy peaks of the Andes mountains. South America contains almost every type of climate and landscape, from lifeless deserts to lush jungles. Annual average temperatures vary from over 80°F (27°C) in the tropical north to below zero in the south. In the east of the region lie some of the wettest places on Earth with an incredible annual rainfall of over 30 feet. In contrast, the Atacama Desert in the west is probably the driest region in the world, with an average annual rainfall of zero. The terrain, which includes glaciers, saltpans, mineral-contaminated lakes, and some of the world's most active volcanoes, is often shaken by major earthquakes.

THE FIRST CIVILIZATIONS

Peru is a very mountainous country that has very little level farming land. The desolate high plains, called *punas*, are too cold to cultivate. The barren coastal plain is mainly desert. The best areas for cultivation and living are the river valleys. About 10,000 years ago, many small communities sprang up along the banks of the rivers which emptied into the Pacific. But there were only six main regions able to support large groups of people.

DEVELOPING SKILLS

The first Andean people lived in stone or mud-brick huts. They ate fish, potatoes, and beans. But as each culture learned from and adopted the ideas of earlier cultures, new skills developed. The first large civilization, the Chavín culture, flourished in the northern highlands of the Andes from about 850 to 350 B.C. The Chavins built terraces for growing crops, storehouses to preserve their harvests, and temples where they worshipped a cat god. Their craftsmen produced many beautiful gold and silver objects.

Chimu goldsmiths at work. They blew through long metal tubes to make the charcoal fire burn hotter. Although the Andean peoples made many wonderful objects in gold, most of them have disappeared— melted down by the Spanish conquistadors.

CRAFTWORK DEVELOPS

On the northern coast of Peru, the Moche culture reached the height of its power about A.D. 800. Their craftworkers made fine pottery, metalwork, and cloth. They built roads and organized a messenger system. The Paracas, to the south, wove elaborate textiles and made unusual terracotta figurines. They also mummified their dead. Further south, the Nazca civilization created mysterious geoglyphs, huge ground drawings that often represented animals.

CITY BUILDERS

The empire of Tiahuanaco grew on the shores of Lake Titicaca from about A.D. 900 to 1300. The Tiahuanacoans were skilled stoneworkers. They built a great religious center with huge temples, giant statues, enormous courtyards, and agricultural terraces. The moon-worshipping Chimus, whose kingdom lasted from about A.D. 1150 to 1450, perfected the art of city-building. The largest of their mud brick cities, Chan Chan, which had a population of 36,000, was probably the most symmetrical city ever built. The Chimus mass-produced pottery, made superb feather tunics, and did large-scale gold-working. But by 1450, all the earlier empires had disappeared. They had been conquered and absorbed by the greatest Andean tribe, the Incas.

A sixth- or seventh-century Mochica clay statue showing a warrior with a club and shield. He wears a helmet over a cloth hood that hides the large plugs he wears in his ears. Inca warriors looked similar to this.

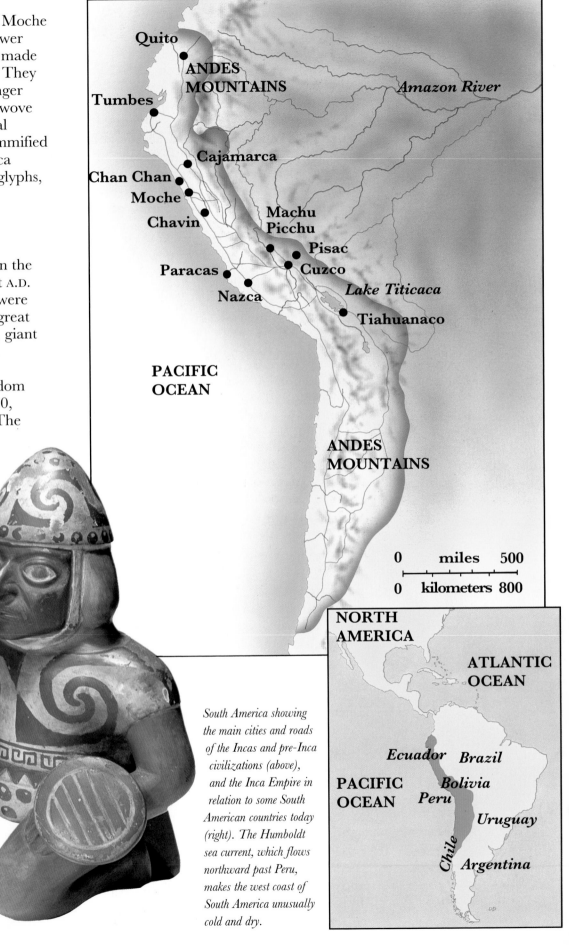

South America showing the main cities and roads of the Incas and pre-Inca civilizations (above), and the Inca Empire in relation to some South American countries today (right). The Humboldt sea current, which flows northward past Peru, makes the west coast of South America unusually cold and dry.

5

THE EMPIRE

No contemporary Inca pictures of Emperor Pachacuti have survived. This picture was drawn by Poma de Ayala, a man of mixed Inca and Spanish blood, over 100 years after Pachacuti died. Most of our written evidence of the Incas comes from Spanish soldiers and priests, or descendants of the Incas writing after the conquest of the Inca empire. Not all of it is completely reliable.

In A.D. 1300 the Incas were a small tribe. During the next 200 years they expanded at a fantastic rate. By 1500, they controlled an empire which rivaled that of ancient Rome. It contained over ten million people and stretched a distance of nearly 2,500 miles down the west coast of South America.

THE FIRST INCAS

The word "Inca" means "lord" in *Quechua*, the Incas' official language, and they used it only to describe their rulers. We now use the word Inca to describe all the people who were ruled by this civilization. The Incas did not have a writing system, so little is known about their early history, which survives today as a blend of truth and legend. It is likely that the tribe settled in a valley high in the Andes where they built their capital, Cuzco, about 1300. At that time, little distinguished the Incas from their warlike neighbors. It was not until after 1438, when Inca Pachacuti became their ruler, that the Incas began to expand their territory at an amazing rate.

THE ALL-CONQUERING INCAS

Pachacuti, the "Earthshaker," seems to have been a military genius. He led spectacular campaigns that massively increased the land area of the developing Inca empire. The rugged Andean landscape, while creating many difficulties for the advancing Incas, also helped them. The tribes who opposed the Incas were scattered over small areas in isolated, steep-sided valleys. These tribes could not join together to resist the Incas who were able to conquer them one by one. With each new conquest, the Inca army grew. As they advanced, the Incas built roads and fortresses to guard their conquests, and storehouses to hold supplies for the army. In this way they were able to keep an iron grip over the areas they conquered.

No obstacle was too great for the Incas to overcome and there must have been many spectacular cliff-top attacks (right). While the Incas had no real technological advantage over their enemies, they had a superior supply system and usually outnumbered their foes.

TOPA YUPANQUI

After about ten years of war, Pachacuti gave his son Topa Yupanqui the task of pursuing the Incas' conquests while he concentrated on ruling his people and rebuilding Cuzco. Topa conquered the highlands and the coastal plains. He even invaded the Amazon rainforest, but here the Incas met their first defeats. They were unable to penetrate the thick jungle. They also met fierce resistance from the Araucanian tribe far to the south. The two sides fought one of the bloodiest battles of medieval times. The battle lasted for three days and left thousands dead or wounded. Eventually the Incas withdrew, accepting the rainforest as the southernmost point of their empire.

THE GROWING EMPIRE

As the campaigns continued, tribes that accepted Inca rule were absorbed peacefully into the empire. Those that did not were conquered or resettled. The Incas demanded that their new subjects follow the Inca way of life. They provided teachers to show the conquered tribes how to build villages, storehouses, and irrigation ditches to improve their agriculture. Enormous quantities of plundered goods flowed back to Cuzco.

GOVERNMENT

While the empire grew, Pachacuti was laying down the foundations of Inca rule. He devised a code of laws that extended Inca control throughout the empire. He standardized the calendar into 12 months of 30 days. He made Sun-worship the official state religion and replaced all non-Inca festivals with new ceremonies for worshipping the Sun. He made himself, as emperor, not only the most powerful person in Peru, but also one of its most important gods. He made Cuzco the spectacular capital of the empire.

The tribespeople of this village have been conquered by the Incas. Peasants are taken as slaves, while the sons of the conquered chief are sent to Cuzco to be trained in the Inca way of ruling. Tribes that could not accept the Inca way of life were sometimes settled elsewhere. Their lands were given to tribes whose loyalty was beyond doubt.

Booty taken from the conquered tribes was sent back to Cuzco. This gold vessel in the shape of a dove was probably used for ceremonial purposes by the Chimu tribe that made it.

7

THE INCA PEOPLE

The subjects of the Inca empire were members of different tribes and ethnic groups which had either been conquered by the Incas or had accepted Inca rule. Most were poor peasants struggling to make a living from the harsh and unforgiving land. United under Inca rule they became one of the most organized and regimented societies that has ever existed.

Each fall the land was divided among the members of the ayllu. Here a newly married couple are leaving a meeting hall after being allocated a piece of land to farm.

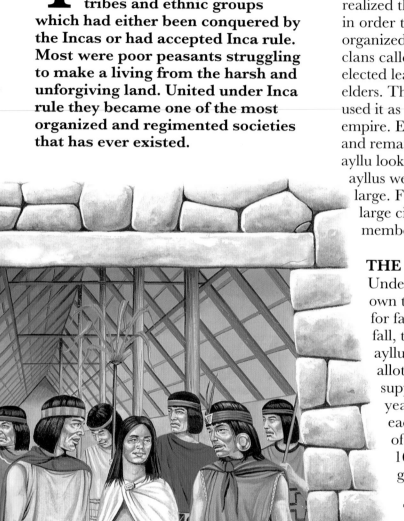

FAMILY GROUPS

From the earliest times the Andean people realized that they needed to work together in order to survive. Many tribes were organized into extended family groups or clans called *ayllus* which were ruled by elected leaders and guided by councils of elders. The Incas adopted the ayllu and used it as the basis for organizing their empire. Everyone was born into an ayllu and remained a lifelong member. Each ayllu looked after its own members. Some ayllus were small; others could be very large. For example, the inhabitants of a large city such as Cuzco were, in effect, members of the same ayllu.

THE DIVISION OF THE LAND

Under Inca rule, each ayllu had its own territory and was responsible for farming the land within it. Every fall, the land was divided among the ayllu's members, all of whom were allotted as much as they needed to support their families for the coming year. In practice this meant that each married couple had a piece of land, or *topo*, roughly 320 by 160 feet. Larger families were given extra land to farm.

TRIBUTE

Each family was responsible for its own piece of land. Some of the land was set aside for the Sapa Inca (the emperor), and some for the Sun God. The peasants worked the Sapa Inca's land and the Sun God's land as a kind of labor tax. About one-third of all the crops and animals produced by an ayllu went as tribute to the Sapa Inca, one-third went to the Sun temples, and about one-third was kept by the ayllu.

The Elderly
60+ years

"Half old"—light work
50–60 years

Able-bodied—hard work
25–50 years

"Almost a youth"—hard work
20–25 years

"Coca-picker"—working
16–20 years

8–16 years

6–8 years

Under 6 years

Able to stand

Baby in arms

The divisions of the ayllu. The main work was done by those aged 16 to 60. The rest were still expected to do whatever work they could manage, however young or old they were.

DIVISION OF THE PEOPLE

Each ayllu was subdivided into groups of "tax-payers." These were the able-bodied people who could pay the labor tax by working on the land and doing craft work. Men also had to pay the *mit'a* (public duty tax) by serving in the army and working on community projects. The groups were based on units of ten—the smallest contained ten people, the largest contained 10,000. In order to distinguish which people were able to pay their taxes, the entire the population was grouped according to age. There were ten categories of men and ten of women. Each group was expected to contribute as much as it could to the community unless the members were too young or too old to be useful.

ADULTHOOD

Once they were 25, men passed into the category of *hatun-runa* or *puric*, meaning able-bodied. They were eligible to pay both the labor tax and the mit'a. Women reached adulthood earlier than men. They looked after the household as well as weaving cloth and helped on the land. Above the age of 60, most men and women were expected to perform only the lightest of duties, such as gathering firewood and babysitting. Once past 80, men and women were given special consideration. They were looked after by other members of the ayllu and could draw what food and clothing they needed from state storehouses, or *qollqas*.

The elderly could draw food and clothing they needed from the state storehouses. The official below is recording the woman's share using a quipu. *In the background, workers are serving their mit'a.*

An original Inca helmet made of woven straw covered with llama wool and cotton. The black square may have been a clan "totem" or symbol. Each Inca tribe had its own totem.

9

THE SAPA INCA

The ruler of the Incas was known as the Sapa Inca. He was thought to be a direct descendant of the Sun and, as such, he was a god. All the land, people, and wealth of the Incas belonged to him. His every command had to be obeyed without question.

THE SUN GOD

His people thought of the Sapa Inca as the Sun God who could be pitiless to his enemies but was always kind to his own people. The Sapa Inca was surrounded by amazing wealth and elaborate ceremony at all times. He ate and drank from golden plates and goblets held by female attendants. Although the Sapa Inca wore clothes similar in style to his subjects, they were of much finer quality. Each day he put on new clothes which had been specially made for him using only the best quality alpaca and vicuña wool. The Sapa Inca was considered so sacred that each day his uneaten food and the clothes from the previous day were laid aside to be ceremonially burned.

GOLDEN THRONE

The Sapa Inca sat on a golden throne. A Spanish chronicler described how visitors to the Sapa Inca's court had to wear burdens strapped to their backs to show him respect. When the Sapa Inca spat, a female servant caught the spittle in her hand. If one of his hairs fell on his clothing, a female servant removed and ate it.

Mummies played an important part in Inca festivals. Most mummies were dried naturally in the dry, cold air of the mountains, without using artificial preservatives. Here some mummies are being paraded during the Festival of the Dead. The mummies were positioned, in order of seniority, and waited on by servants.

The Sapa Inca on his throne with various symbols of his authority, including a royal headdress made of wool. The Sapa Inca sometimes carried a small banner made of stiffened cloth which may have been a kind of scepter.

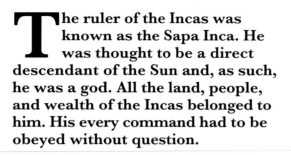

OFFICIAL HISTORY

When the Sapa Inca died, the entire empire went into mourning. A council decided what memories of his life should be preserved. These were then recorded on *quipus* and became the official history. Rememberers were instructed what to say about the dead lord. The destruction of quipus by Spanish priests, who thought they were the books of the devil, as well as the dying out of rememberers, resulted in much Inca history being lost.

MUMMY WORSHIP

So that the Sapa Inca could attain eternal life, his body was preserved through a process known as mummification. His personal servants were ceremonially strangled so they could serve their ruler in the afterlife.

But the old ruler was not thought of as dead. The royal mummies were regarded as visible links between the people and the gods, and were kept in great luxury as symbols of life after death. The Sapa Inca's house in Cuzco became a shrine. Each Sapa Inca's mummy was served with food as if it were still alive. It played an important part in many religious ceremonies. Mummies were even taken to visit each other!

The dead toasted one another, and they drank to the living and vice versa; this was done by their ministers in their names.

— *Bernabé Cobo* —

THE PANACA

Except for the son chosen as his successor, all of the Sapa Inca's male descendants became courtiers of the dead Inca. This family group of attendants was called a *panaca*.

The panaca system had a great effect on the new Sapa Inca. He inherited the throne and tremendous power but no land, because the panaca of the previous ruler managed all the royal property, including its palaces, lands, and servants. The Sapa Inca's wealth came from his lands and from the labor tax he collected on it. In order to increase the number of people paying the labor tax, the Sapa Inca needed more land. Without land, an Inca ruler could not govern and, even more important, could not amass wealth for his own panaca. This system might help to explain the rapid expansion of the Inca empire, since each new Sapa Inca was compelled to conquer new land for himself and his panaca.

This golden mask is shaped to represent the Sun God. In theory, all gold in the empire belonged to the Sapa Inca.

THE GOVERNMENT

A quipu was a bundle of knotted cords used by the Incas to keep records. The key to how quipus worked has been lost but the position, color, and length of the cords, as well as the number and size of the knots, are believed to represent numbers, words, and ideas.

The Inca emperors ruled an enormous empire, which they called *Tahuantinsuyu*, or the Land of the Four Quarters. They did this without the benefit of a writing system, knowledge of the wheel, or iron tools. In spite of these disadvantages, the government was highly organized and Inca laws rigidly enforced. Punishments for committing crimes could be severe.

PACHACUTI'S LAWS

Inca laws derived from their various traditions, customs, and taboos. In order to govern all reaches of the growing empire effectively, Pachacuti simplified and reorganized the laws about 1450. His laws were administered by the officials who had been appointed to control each group of people.

THE PYRAMID STATE

Inca society was organized like a pyramid. At the top was the Sapa Inca. He was the emperor, chief priest, commander-in-chief, and son of the Sun God.

Under the Sapa Inca were two classes of nobles. The first class were true-blood Incas; relatives of the Sapa Inca who were descended from the Inca dynasty. The second class were nobles by privilege, or "adopted" Incas. They were often local rulers who had earned the Sapa Inca's trust. The most important nobles administered the Sapa Inca's far-flung lands, acting as his eyes and ears.

In court each party told their story to a curaca who then passed judgement. Sentences could be reduced for murderers who killed in self-defense or lost control through anger.

This group of pottery figures shows a drunken Inca being helped by his neighbors. People often got drunk during festivals by drinking ceremonial beer called chicha. *Drunkenness was not considered a crime in Inca society.*

THE CURACAS

The Inca Empire had expanded so rapidly that there were not enough pure Incas to rule it. When a new territory was overrun, the Incas sometimes allowed the chiefs of the conquered tribes to continue governing. These chiefs were known as *curacas*, and held important administrative posts in the empire. The sons of the chiefs were taken away to Cuzco to learn Quecha and to be taught how to rule in the Inca way. Inca nobles and curacas did not pay any taxes.

Beneath the curacas were lesser officials known as the *caramayoc* (village headmen). They were responsible for enforcing the law at a local level. Each headman was responsible for a certain number of peasant households.

In order to rule efficiently, the Sapa Inca had to know what was happening inside his empire. One of the ways this was achieved was by carrying out regular censuses. The results were recorded on quipus. In this way the Sapa Inca knew all the resources of the empire. The censuses were carried out by the emperor's envoy, called a runaquipa.

HARSH PUNISHMENTS

Because crimes against the state were considered crimes against the Sapa Inca, and thus against the Sun God, punishments were very harsh. There was no system of imprisonment. Instead, a first offense for a minor crime might result in a public scolding. Second offenses could lead to death by hanging, stoning, or by pushing the offender over a cliff. The death penalty was given for murder, stealing, breaking into state storage chambers, damaging bridges, or entering the rooms of Chosen Women. Laziness, which was considered a very serious crime since lazy people deprived the Sapa Inca of their work, was also punishable by death. The upper classes were punished more severely than the peasants, because more was expected from them. Public humiliation for the common people was replaced by banishment for the nobility. Where ordinary taxpayers might be tortured or mutilated, nobles would be put to death.

Pushing a criminal off a cliff was a form of execution that had been used by Indian tribes in the Andes for hundreds, if not thousands, of years.

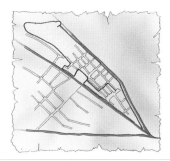

A plan of Cuzco, showing its shape like a crouching puma. The city, which housed about 100,000 people, was cleaner and better maintained than most European cities of the same time. The festival held to celebrate the city's founding took place in spring. First, the city was "cleansed" of evil spirits. Royal princes carrying spears chased the spirits out of the city along the four main roads (below). Outside the city, the lances were driven into the ground. These formed a barrier which would keep evil spirits away for another year.

The city of Cuzco lay in a mountain valley about 13,000 feet above sea level. Cuzco, which means "navel" in the Inca language, was rebuilt by Pachacuti and made the center of his empire.

PACHACUTI'S DESIGN

Pachacuti restored the palaces of former emperors and built a magnificent one for himself, called the *Cassana*. He designed and built the *Accla Huasi*, the house of the 4,000 Chosen Women of the Sun God. He laid out gardens filled with trees, flowers, and herbs. Each year a festival was held to celebrate the founding of the city. The festival coincided with celebrations of the arrival of spring. First, the Sapa Inca hailed the Sun God. Next, royal princes chased evil spirits out of the city. Later, ritual bathing got rid of any remaining evil, and everyone danced and sang all night. Finally people rubbed their bodies and houses with *sanko* (corn paste) to ward off illness and weakness.

REFLECTION OF THE EMPIRE

The city was divided into four quarters that echoed the division of the empire; so, for example, people from the eastern part of the empire lived in the eastern part of the city. The curacas built their homes in the correct quarter surrounded by their subjects. Walking through the city was like walking through the empire.

THE CITY OF THE PUMA

The inner city of Cuzco was laid out in the shape of a puma. The head of the puma was the fortress of Sacsahuamán (which means "imperial falcon") in the north of the city, and the tail was a public garden in the south. The heart was the *Huacapata*, or holy square, containing the Coricancha, or Temple of the Sun. Within the puma was a grid of paved streets, each with a stone gutter carrying fresh mountain water. These helped citizens keep their homes clean and sanitary. In addition, people regularly bathed in the Huatanay and the Tullumayo rivers, which flowed along either flank of the puma. Only members of the royal ayllu and the most important citizens lived in the inner city. Ordinary citizens lived in the suburbs outside the puma.

SACSAHUAMÁN

The city was guarded by the fortress of Sacsahuamán, which was built into the steep-sided hill that overlooked Cuzco. The south face of the hill was a sheer cliff. The other sides of the city were guarded by gigantic terraced walls that rose one above the other. Sacsahuamán contained an arsenal, a temple, parade-grounds, palaces, vaults, reservoirs, storerooms, and the throne of the Sapa Inca. Invading Spaniards were awestruck by the fortress.

Many who have visited it, and who have traveled in Lombardy and other foreign countries, say they have never seen a building to compare with it. Nothing built by the Romans is as impressive as this.

— Sancho —

The fortress of Sacsahuamán stood on a hill above Cuzco. The remains of part of the enormous zig-zag walls with their doorways can be seen in this view.

OBSERVATORIES

The Incas also built simple astronomical observatories. Priests used these to observe the sun and planets. This helped them calculate the passing of the seasons so that the farming cycle of plowing, planting, and harvesting could proceed at the right times. Many observatories consisted of a single pillar placed to allow priests to measure the progress of the sun through the sky. Others were more elaborate.

An Inca observatory. The Spaniards described how the observatories in Cuzco consisted of eight stone pillars on the eastern side of the city, and eight on the western side. These were organized into two rows of four and stood about 23 feet apart on specially raised and leveled ground. On the tops of the pillars were discs through which the sun's rays could pass. Lines drawn on the ground marked the passage of the sun across the sky.

15

PALACE ON THE LAKE

The see-through scene below shows the Palace of the Inca and the Temple of the Chosen Women on islands on Lake Titicaca. The reconstructions are based on a few remains on the islands and descriptions of Spanish chroniclers and later travelers. In reality, the islands were several miles apart. On the lake, a procession of reed boats sails by. In the distance are the floating homes of Uru tribespeople, built on islands made of reeds.

While Cuzco was the center of government, Lake Titicaca was the legendary birthplace of the first Incas. One Inca myth tells of a great flood after which the first rays of the Sun fell on one of the islands. Here the Sun created his children, the Incas.

LAKE OF THE JAGUAR

Lake Titicaca is the highest navigable lake in the world. At 12,500 feet above sea level, those unused to the thin air gasp for breath at the slightest effort. No one is sure what Titicaca means. Some people believe it means Wild Cat Lake or, perhaps, Lake of the Jaguar. The lake is about 120 miles long and contains 25 islands. On the lake's shores lived the Uru tribe which had been absorbed into the Inca Empire.

ISLAND OF THE SUN

The most important part of the lake was an island that the Incas called the Island of the Sun. The island contained a single temple called the Palace of the Inca. This was a two-story building, about 52 by 46 feet. Although it was small, the temple contained fabulous wealth. It stands at the point legend claims was the birthplace of the first Incas. It is probable that the Sapa Inca made an annual pilgrimage there.

At one end of Lake Titicaca there was a bridge that crossed a river flowing into the lake. This drawing is based on a sketch made by a Spanish chronicler.

SACRED CORN

The rest of the island was transformed by terracing into a vast garden. Here priests cultivated sacred corn kernels. The harvest from these was considered a symbol of the fertility of the entire empire. The corn was distributed every year to all the temples throughout the empire.

THE ISLAND OF THE MOON

Many Andean people, particularly those who lived in the hot, lower regions and feared the fierce heat of the sun, worshipped the moon instead. Both Sun and Moon worship seem to have been practiced at Lake Titicaca. The moon was worshipped at Coati, the Island of the Moon, which was next to the Island of the Sun. This contained a much larger building which is known as the Temple of the Moon and was probably an *acclahausi* (home) for Chosen Women serving the Moon God. Unlike most Inca buildings, the walls were coated with mud plaster. Shapes and decorations were pressed into the mud and the entire building was painted yellow and red.

Corn was thought to be sacred by the Incas and was cultivated on the Island of the Sun. The Spanish conquerors were astounded to discover that the gardens around Coricancha in Cuzco were planted with lifesize corn stalks made of gold and silver, similar to the one shown here.

1 **Island of the Moon**
2 **Temple of the Chosen Women**
3 **Stepped niches**
4 **Island of the Sun**
5 **Palace of the Inca**
6 **Corbelled vaults**
7 **Reed boats**
8 **Uru floating islands**

ENGINEERING THE LAND

A partially restored building. Notice the clean rockface at the top where stone was split away. The face may have been smoothed with sand. The walls below have been repaired with modern cement, but the shapes of the stones can be clearly seen.

Inca stoneworkers split blocks of stone from the rockface with wooden wedges. These were shaped with stone or obsidian tools and moved around by brute force. Great public works such as temples took years to build.

The Incas were very skillful engineers who learned how to manipulate the land to suit their needs. Using only the simplest tools and massive human effort, they created public works that amaze engineers today.

TERRACING

Much of the land in the Inca Empire was hard to farm. In places where there was sufficient rainfall, the ground sloped too steeply for farming, and the rain washed the soil away. Where the land was flat enough to work, there was too little rainfall. So the Incas increased the amount of farming land in two main ways. The first, and most spectacular, was by terracing the hillsides. The second was by digging canals to irrigate (water) the land.

All major engineering projects were planned by professional architects sent from Cuzco. All the work was done by hand. Elaborate terracing transformed steep hillsides into huge flights of stone steps that supported flat fields. These greatly increased the amount of land that could be farmed, and also stopped the rain from washing away the soil.

A typical piece of Inca stonework. The perfect joints between each differently shaped stone took many hours to shape.

IRRIGATION

In areas where rain was scarce, engineers built reservoirs and cisterns to store water. Many of these were underground and lined with stone to prevent the water from evaporating. An elaborate network of canals and ditches carried water from wetter areas and mountain streams to irrigate the fields and fill the cisterns. The engineers also built dams and straightened rivers to improve the flow of water and reduce erosion of the fertile banks.

SCIENTIFIC KNOWLEDGE

These works indicate that the Incas had a good knowledge of practical science. Inca engineers were able to introduce water on the top step of a terrace and direct it to run down, watering each of the steps below in turn. They knew that water flowing too fast could erode the banks of a stream and that water flowing too slowly would allow weeds to grow, which in turn could block a channel.

To make the land more productive, they used the huge deposits of guano (bird droppings) found along the coast as fertilizer. They considered this resource so valuable that killing seabirds became a crime punishable by death!

BUILDING

Nowhere is the skill of the Incas better represented than in their buildings. By 1500, the empire contained an enormous number of stone buildings, even in cities like Machu Picchu, high up in the mountains. These were created by countless hours of back-breaking work.

Inca workers quarried the stone by hand in much the same manner as the ancient Egyptians. They enlarged natural faults in the rockface by inserting wet wooden wedges that swelled to crack the rock. The blocks that split off the rockface were dragged to the building site using rollers, levers, sledges, and ropes. When high walls or terraces were being built, the Incas made earth ramps up which the massive stone blocks could be pulled. These were then levered into place.

SHAPING STONE

Inca masons shaped the blocks with stone axes and obsidian pebbles, and smoothed the edges with sand. Using these simple tools, the Incas produced impressive stonework with joints so tight that not even the thinnest knife could be driven in. The stones were not regular in shape and no two were quite the same size. They had many faces and some had as many as 30 corners. Yet in every Inca building all the stones interlock precisely. Each stone, even those weighing many tons, must have been tried in place time after time to test the fit.

Remains of buildings in the Inca city of Pisac. The ruins in the foreground were once a sacred ceremonial center. The Incas learned their craft from cultures that had developed stoneworking before they did.

In some areas, the Incas made adobe (mud bricks) using wooden molds. This was a much quicker way of building houses, though the results were less permanent.

FOOD AND FARMING

Inca farms were usually situated midway between the valleys and highland pastures. The peasant farmers could therefore grow more than one food crop and also raise animals. This helped them vary their diet and avoid starvation if a whole crop was lost. Any surplus foods were stored in qollqas, ready for distribution by officials when food became scarce.

STAPLE FOODS

While all Incas depended on certain staple (basic) foods, what they ate depended on the area where they lived. In mountainous regions, the staple food was the potato. When the potatoes had been harvested, they were left outside at night to freeze. Then they were dried in the hot sun. This process of freeze-drying produced *chuñu*, a food that could be stored for long periods. At lower altitudes, the Incas grew corn, which also could be kept for long periods and eaten when other foods were scarce.

Inca farmers used the taclla *or foot-plow to dig the ground. The men stood in lines moving backwards as they dug up the earth with their plows. The women crouched in front of the men, breaking up the earth with hoes called* lampas, *and planting.*

The Incas used reed boats when fishing on inland waters. Boats like this are still used today. The Incas used rafts made from balsa wood to make sea journeys.

THE FARMING YEAR

There were two main seasons in the farming year: the wet season (from October to May), and the dry season (from June to September). The times for planting, harvesting, and tilling the soil followed a strict pattern. August, the month for plowing, always began with a festival in which the nobles played an important role.

If the Sapa Inca himself or his governor or some high official happened to be present, he started the work with a golden digging stick which they brought to the Inca, and following his example all the other officials and nobles who accompanied him did the same.

Padre Coba

A VARIED DIET

Many of the foods we enjoy now, such as avocados, peppers, tomatoes, and chocolate, were first produced by Andean farmers. Coca and a barley-like grain called *quinoa* were grown in some parts of the empire. In tropical areas, the Incas grew guavas and cactus. People who lived near the coasts caught and dried fish. Wildfowl, such as duck, were eaten, and most people kept guinea pigs for meat.

MEALS

Most Incas began their day with a snack at dawn. They drank *a'ka*, a thick, mildly alcoholic, malty drink and ate what was left of the previous evening's supper. They ate a substantial meal at midday. The Incas did not know how to fry, and boiled most of their food. A favorite dish was *mote* which was corn cooked with peppers and herbs. Sun-dried llama meat and powdered chuñu was made into a stew called *locro*. They baked a kind of bread made from ground corn and cooked in the ashes of the fire. They knew how to make popcorn and thought it a delicacy.

FORMAL MEALS

Supper was eaten between four and five o'clock. The food was placed in cooking pots on a cloth on the ground. The men squatted around and helped themselves. They ate with their fingers, although they would drink soup from bowls. The women, who had done all the cooking, sat outside the circle with their backs to the men. An important guest, such as a curaca, would sit in a place of honor.

An Inca pot made of clay, used to carry water. The long narrow neck makes it harder to spill the water and easier to pour it out.

21

THE ROLE OF WOMEN

Women played a vital role in Inca society. They acted as wives, mothers, servants, farmers, and attendants of the Sun God. But like all Incas they had little choice about what they did. The Inca state decided which careers women would follow. Once they had been set on their chosen paths, there was little opportunity to turn back.

An Inca marriage ceremony. The couples were married in a simple ceremony of holding hands and exchanging sandals.

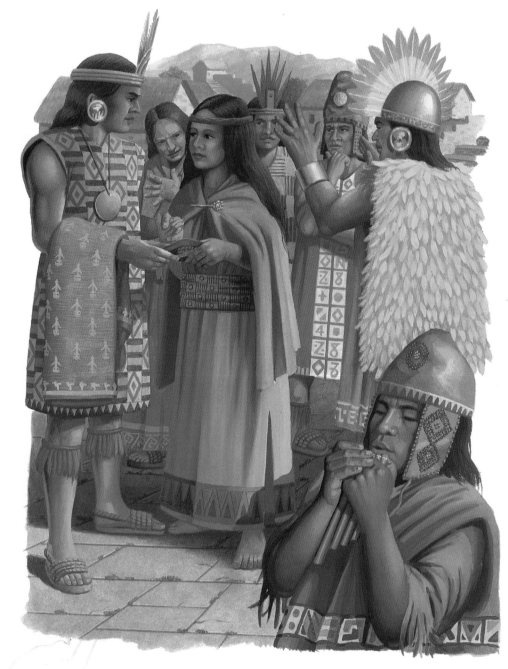

THE LEFT-OUT GIRLS

About the age of ten, Inca girls were judged on their social rank and beauty and put into one of two groups at the annual census. The visiting runaquipa sent the most beautiful girls away to be trained as *acllacunas*, or Chosen Women. The other group, known as "left-out" girls, remained in their villages. Here they learned all the skills they would need in life, particularly spinning, weaving, and cooking.

MARRIAGE

When they became 12 years old, the "left-out" girls were considered old enough to marry. Every year, the curaca held a marriage market where husbands were chosen for them. All boys who had reached the age of 24 had to attend the market. The couples were married in a simple ceremony of holding hands and exchanging sandals. The women spent the rest of their lives classed as "warriors' wives," raising their families and helping with the farming.

THE CHOSEN WOMEN

Girls selected as Chosen Women trained for lives as priestesses and servants to the Sapa Inca. There were as many as 15,000 Chosen Women in the empire at any one time. The girls were trained in *mamacona* institutes, which were similar to convents and situated near towns. The largest, near Cuzco, contained almost 1,500 women.

LEARNING DUTIES

The girls were supervised by older, unmarried Chosen Women called *mamaconas*, who were considered wives of the Sun God. The girls learned about the rituals surrounding the Sun religion. They also learned how to cook and to weave vicuña wool into the best quality cloth, called *cumbi*. The mamaconas made clothes from the cumbi, which could only be worn by the Sapa Inca and his chief wife (who was known as the *coya*).

PRIESTESSES OF THE SUN

Their training over, the girls were divided again. Many became priestesses called the Handmaidens of the Sun. They were sent to temples of the Sun where they assisted in the worship of all the Inca's gods, although they mainly served the Sun God. They prepared ceremonial food and drink, especially the beer called chicha which was drunk in large amounts during festivals. A few Chosen Women were singled out to be sacrificed. This was considered a great honor.

Domestic chores like cooking and spinning were done by women. Here a young woman is grinding corn cobs into flour using a heavy stone handmill. Behind her, another woman is spinning wool that has been washed and combed.

NOBLE WIVES

Some of the Chosen Women became the wives or concubines of high officials or famous generals, members of the royal ayllu. Some were sent to the House of the Inca's Chosen Women. Here they became the wives of the Sapa Inca himself. Most Sapa Incas had hundreds of wives. Atahualpa was reported to have had 700.

As a result, each Sapa Inca had many descendants from whom he could chose his court, his chief administrators, and his successor. All of the Inca's sons were considered to be of equal rank and the eldest son did not necessarily become the next Sapa Inca. This led to many plots and revolts in the royal family, particularly at the start of a new reign, as each son might try to gain power.

Handmaidens of the Sun tended the sacred fire inside the Sun temples. There were sun temples throughout the empire. The handmaidens lived protected lives much like nuns', watched over by senior priestesses.

The coya was the most important of all the Sapa Inca's wives. She was waited on hand and foot by the daughters of nobles. This illustration of a Sapa Inca's coya was drawn by Poma de Ayala in 1620.

KEEPING POWER

The most important woman in the Inca empire was the Sapa Inca's sister. This was because the Sapa Inca married his own sister, taking her as his chief wife, the coya, which means "star." She was the only legitimate wife of the Sapa Inca, and she lived a life of great luxury. Only the Sapa Inca was allowed to marry his sister. In this way he ensured that his divinity was passed on to his descendants.

23

HOUSES AND HOMES

O rdinary Incas spent most of their lives outside, working. What little spare time they had was occupied by eating and sleeping. Therefore most of their homes were simple shelters designed to protect them from the worst effects of the cold, rain, and snow. As good farming land was scarce, houses were usually built on rocky or barren land where crops could not be grown.

HOUSES

Most Incas lived in rectangular houses built of adobe bricks or rocks plastered with mud. The roof was held up with wooden poles. Most houses had a single window and one door that were simple openings in the wall covered with wool curtains. The roof was thickly thatched with grass. Inside, the floor was bare earth. On this was a simple hearth made from stones arranged in a rough circle. There was no chimney, and the smoke from the cooking fire drifted out through the thatched roof.

PERSONAL BELONGINGS

Houses had no real furniture. People sat or slept on llama skins, wool blankets, or reed mats. Some houses had stone benches built into the walls and niches which held small statues of Inca gods. Incas used pegs to hang up their possessions. If the husband was a warrior, he would hang up his warrior's fighting tunic, his helmet, and his shield which would be decorated with his ayllu's totem (badge). Ordinary peasants did not own very much, but they might each have had an extra tunic, a shawl, a decorated cloak for wearing at festivals, and a sling.

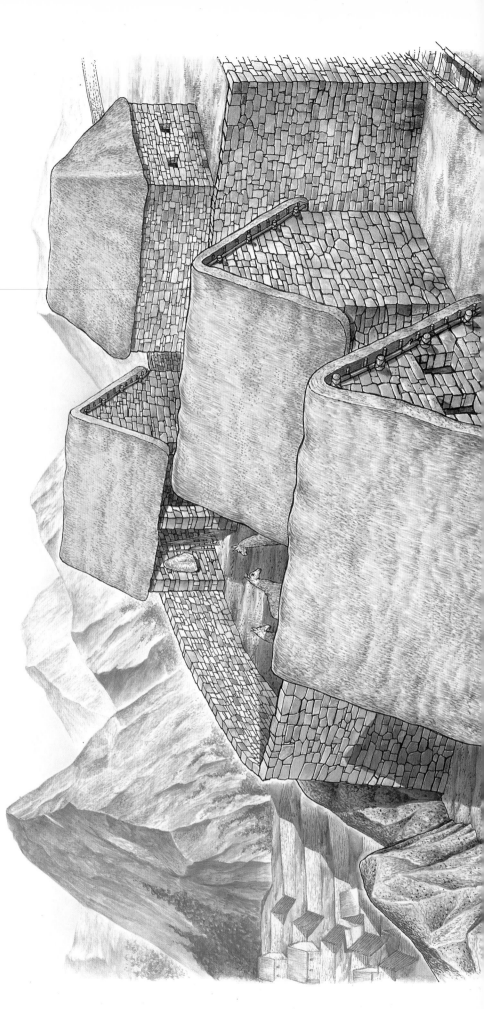

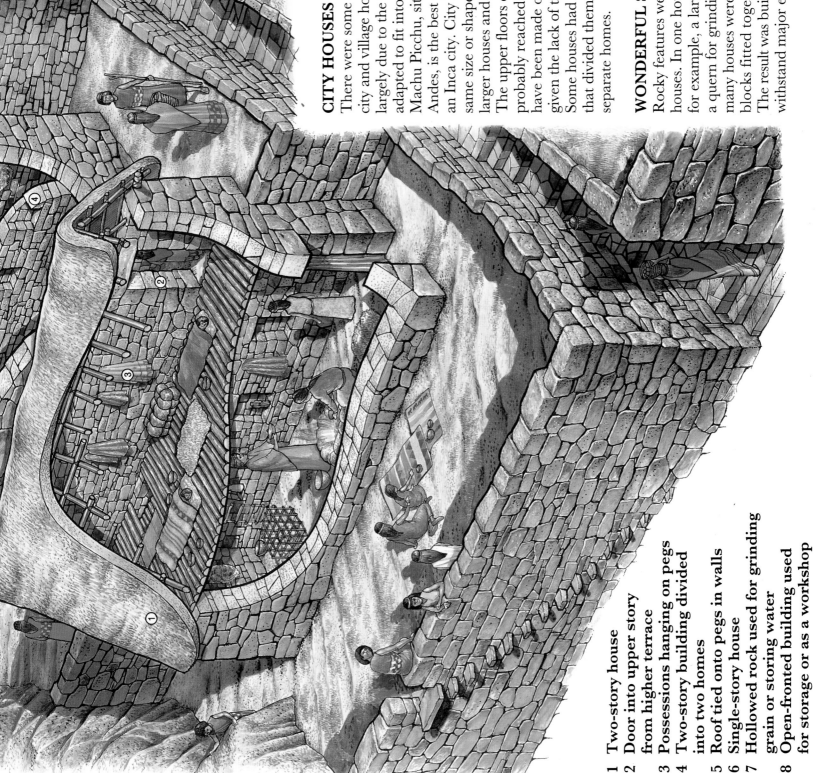

CITY HOUSES

There were some differences between city and village houses. These were largely due to the way city houses were adapted to fit into the available space. Machu Picchu, situated high up in the Andes, is the best preserved example of an Inca city. City houses were not all the same size or shape. There were some larger houses and some with two stories. The upper floors of houses were probably reached by a ladder. This may have been made of rope instead of wood, given the lack of trees at this altitude. Some houses had a lengthwise stone wall that divided them into two completely separate homes.

WONDERFUL STONEWORK

Rocky features were built into some houses. In one house at Machu Picchu, for example, a large rock was carved into a quern for grinding grain. The walls of many houses were built of shaped stone blocks fitted together without mortar. The result was buildings that were able to withstand major earthquakes.

1 Two-story house
2 Door into upper story
   from higher terrace
3 Possessions hanging on pegs
4 Two-story building divided
   into two homes
5 Roof tied onto pegs in walls
6 Single-story house
7 Hollowed rock used for grinding
   grain or storing water
8 Open-fronted building used
   for storage or as a workshop

ARTS AND CRAFTS

An Inca featherwork fan. Many of the brightly colored feathers the Incas used to make their intricate feather mosaics and other types of featherwork came from birds caught in the Amazon jungle.

Almost everyone in Inca society did some kind of craftwork. Like all activities within the Inca Empire, the work was highly organized. Though some craftwork was done at home, much of it was done by groups of workers in large work areas like factories.

TEXTILES
Cloth-making was probably the most important craft activity. Cotton was grown in the lowlands, but wool was the main Andean material. Alpaca wool, easy to work with because of its fine quality, was used to make *awaka*, the most widely used type of cloth. Awaka was usually white, mixed with grays and natural browns. Llama wool, which was coarse and greasy, was spun as fiber for blankets, sacks, ropes, and llama halters. The best quality cloth came from vicuña wool, which was soft and silky.

This pottery figure shows an Inca porter carrying a bottle-shaped pot called an aryballos. *The pot would balance perfectly on its pointed bottom when full.*

Most Inca garments were made by joining rectangular pieces of cloth together, as in this poncho. The hole for the head was simply a slit or slits where the material was not joined.

MAKING THE CLOTH
After the animals had been sheared, the wool was divided among members of the ayllu. Any surplus was stored in official storage bins at the qollqas. Although Incas often used raw wool, they were skilled in the art of dyeing. They dyed much of the wool before spinning it. They also knew how to tie-dye the finished cloth, producing a pattern of brilliant colors. Dyes came from plants and from dried cochineal insects which produced a vivid red.

The thread was spun on drop spindles fitted with ceramic whorls. Weaving was done by both men and women, although women worked with the finest wools. Most cloth was woven on a backstrap, or belt loom. One end of the cloth was tied around a tree or other upright object and the other end was tied around the weaver's back. The weavers kept the cloth taut by leaning backward as they wove.

FANCY CLOTH

Some skilled workers made tunics from the brilliantly-colored feathers of jungle birds, such as parrots or macaws. They also made cloth called *cahquira* which was decorated with bangles of gold or tiny bells and golden specks. Some tunics were completely covered with gold, silver, or burnished copper pieces. Tunics such as these were worn by the highest nobles at feasts or religious festivals.

POTTERY

The Incas were skillful potters. They were able to make pottery, some of which was very delicate, without using a potter's wheel. The Inca potter rolled the clay into oblong shapes and coiled them to make a pot. The sides of the pot were smoothed with a small wooden tool shaped like a spatula. The pots were dried in the sun, painted with geometric or animal designs, and then fired to harden them.

Inca pottery was both practical and decorative. Potters made three-legged pots which were used by soldiers on campaign and large, elegant pots, similar to Grecian urns. Another popular design was the whistling pot. When the pot was emptied, air was drawn in, making a whistling sound. These pots often showed a person playing a flute or a whistle.

THE SWEAT OF THE SUN

The Incas produced huge quantities of gold and silver, which they called "sweat of the Sun" and "tears of the Moon." Most of the gold was found in rivers, by washing it out of river gravel (panning). The Incas also mined for gold and silver in the mountains. It has been estimated that as much as 220 tons of gold was produced annually. Many Incas paid their labor tax by working in the mines, digging for precious metals.

THE SAPA INCA'S GOLD

Each grain of metal mined or panned was recorded on quipus. Precious metals belonged to the Sapa Inca and had to be sent to Cuzco. Here goldsmiths used many different methods to work the metal. They made a huge number of gold objects. Important buildings were often sheathed in gold panels. After the death of a Sapa Inca, a life-size gold statue was made of him. His palace, which became his tomb, was ornamented in gold. The Spanish reported seeing gardens filled with plants, trees, and animals all made of gold. Sadly, few of these wonderful golden objects have survived since the Spanish conquerors melted most of them down.

This silver figurine of a woman chewing coca leaves is a fine example of the skill of Inca silversmiths.

Women weaving llama wool on backstrap looms. These portable looms were used in many parts of Central and South America.

CLOTHES AND FASHION

Noble Incas wore golden ear plugs. The ones above show a warrior carrying a spear and shield, picked out in semi-precious stones.

The clothes worn by the Incas, from the most powerful noble to the humblest worker, were very similar in style. Nevertheless, there were many variations in the colors, patterns, and quality of the garments. However, where people lived had more effect on what they wore. In the high mountains, for example, the Incas wore many layers of clothes made principally from alpaca wool. In the warmer lowlands, light clothes made from cotton were more practical.

This rich Inca family is preparing to attend a festival. Though the clothes worn by the Incas were similar in style and shape, only noble Incas would have worn clothes as fine as these.

MEN'S CLOTHES

All Inca men wore a loincloth, which was a length of cloth worn around the waist. It was made of cotton or wool and held in place by a colorful belt made of woven wool. Over this many Inca men wore a tunic. This was a simple garment, usually made of alpaca wool, that looked like a poncho. During cold weather or in higher areas an Inca wrapped himself in a *yacolla*, or cape, which was also made of wool. He wore sandals on his feet, and braided his hair with colored strings. During festivals, men wore highly decorated tunics that reached down to their ankles.

WOMEN'S CLOTHES

All Inca women dressed in the *anacu*. This was an ankle-length tunic, woven from alpaca wool. It was gathered at the waist with a sash. Over this the woman wore a shawl that she fastened with a *tupu*, a copper, silver, or gold pin, depending on her rank in society. Women wore their long hair parted in the middle or braided and tied with colored ribbons. Like the men, they wore sandals on their feet.

Inca tunics. The cantuta flowers on the white poncho were popular in Inca times and are now the state emblem of Peru. The base of the poncho on the left is woven cloth into which the quills of hundreds of feathers have been pushed. The design, which shows birds, is created by using feathers of different colors. A cloak as magnificent as this would have been worn by someone very important.

This tupu pin was found at Sacsahuamán. The Incas did not have buttons. They used straps, laces, and pins like this to hold their clothes together.

NOBLES' CLOTHING

Although Inca nobles dressed in a similar style to the ordinary workers, their garments were of much better quality. Their tunics and loincloths were woven from the finest vicuña wool. On special occasions they wore more exotic garments, such as mantles made from dyed birds' feathers. The Sapa Inca, Atahualpa, was described by one of the Spanish conquistadors (conquerors) as wearing a dark mantle made of bat skins.

SYMBOLS OF AUTHORITY

Eminent Incas wore or carried special objects as symbols of their authority. The Sapa Inca carried a golden-headed mace, which was decorated with a pennant, and wore a crown called a *llautu* with a fringe of red tassels that hung above his eyes. An official called a *totrioc michoc*, whose job it was to rule the provinces and act as judge, had earlobes that were split open to hang down the sides of his cheeks. Feather headdresses and gold jewelry marked out other important officials, such as priests.

PIERCED EARS

Noble Incas could often be distinguished by the large ear plugs they wore. The plugs were usually made of gold. Noble men pierced their ears at an early age and wore rounded golden and jeweled disks in the holes. Gradually the size of these ear plugs was increased. This stretched the holes until they became large enough to pass an egg through.

Ear plugs showed the status of their wearer. The larger and more splendid the ear plugs, the more important the wearer. The Spaniards called some priests *orejones*, which meant "big ears," after their huge ear plugs. The Sapa Inca had the most splendid and enormous ear plugs of all.

This rectangular bag was made of wool and decorated with small gold plates. It was worn slung over the shoulder.

GROWING UP

An 11th–13th century Chancay doll made from woven cloth. Inca children would have played with dolls similar to this.

An Inca mother places her baby in its wooden cradle. The baby was strapped tightly in. The cradle could be left on the ground or slung on the mother's back so the baby was carried in a vertical position looking backward.

Children were trained from birth for their future role in the community. For most this meant learning to suffer cold and hunger without complaint, and to obey all orders. A stern upbringing may have been thought to help prepare them for any hardship they might experience as adults.

BIRTH AND INFANCY

There were no Inca midwives to help deliver babies. In a typical delivery, a mother gave birth, washed herself and her baby in a nearby stream, and then returned to work. This no-fuss beginning set the pattern for Inca childhood. A few days after birth, the baby was placed in a cradle, or *quirau*, and carried around on its mother's back. For the first two years of its life, a child was likely to be called simply *wawa*, or baby.

A COLD START

Babies were washed in cold water every morning, then wrapped tightly in cloth. The cold dip was believed to strengthen the child's arms and legs and help it withstand the mountain climate. Babies were nursed until they were two or three years old.

According to Garcilaso de la Vega, babies were fed at regular intervals. He said they were never fed "on demand," and did not seem to have been cuddled much by their mothers. Soon after it stopped breastfeeding, a baby received a ritual haircut called *rutuchicoy*, and was given a temporary name that often recalled the circumstances of its birth, such as Thunderstorm.

EARLY YEARS

When a baby was not in its cradle, it was sometimes kept in a hole dug in the ground that acted like a playpen. During the first two years of a child's life Inca parents were allowed to look after their children, but they did not play with them much. Children were expected to learn to crawl and walk without any help.

While they may not have been lavished with attention, babies were always looked after. Even unwanted babies were not simply abandoned by their mothers. The Incas had a number of state orphanages where unwanted babies could be cared for.

LEARNING USEFUL SKILLS

Once a child was two years old it was classified as a member of the group of "bread receivers." Children were still allowed to play, but they now had to learn useful skills and begin to take on responsibilities. Punishments for children who misbehaved could be very severe. Most of the lessons were learned from older members of the ayllu. Peasant children were probably taught the various Inca customs and taboos. The sons of nobles had tutors called *amataus*. They were taught the main rites and beliefs of Sun worship, the chief laws, and given some instruction in politics and military matters.

Having endured tests of his courage, a noble boy swears loyalty to the Sapa Inca and receives his first sling, shield, and mace.

BECOMING AN ADULT

At puberty, a boy was given a permanent name. When he was 14 he attended the most important ceremony of his life at which he received his loincloth. This symbolized becoming a man. The sons of nobles went on a pilgrimage to the birth-place of the Inca state in the Cuzco valley. There, each boy had to endure tests of his courage, strength, and discipline. He attended various religious ceremonies during which llamas were sacrificed and blood was smeared on his face. He swore an oath of loyalty to the Sapa Inca and received his sling, shield, and mace. At the end of the sixth day the boy's ears were pierced, his first ear plugs were inserted and he officially became a warrior in the Sapa Inca's elite guards.

PREPARING FOR MARRIAGE

Young girls came of age and were named at about the same age as boys. This occasion was marked with a hair-combing ceremony. Girls married soon after this.

By the time a male descendant of the Sapa Inca was ready to marry, he had received as thorough an education as possible in a land without schools. He had gone with the Sapa Inca on tours of the empire, fought in battles, learned the important rituals of Sun worship, and heard the most important stories in Inca history.

This simple pottery model shows a mother holding her baby as she carries a huge pot on her back.

TEMPLES OF THE SUN

The Incas had many gods, beliefs and superstitions. In addition to worshipping the Sun God and a host of other gods, they believed that everyone had a *hauqui*, or guardian spirit. They revered holy objects and places they called *huacas*. Each ayllu had its own huaca. Coricancha, the Temple of the Sun in Cuzco, was the huaca for the whole empire.

GODS

Viracocha was the god of creation, but the most widely worshipped and powerful god was *Inti*, the Sun God. Inti gave heat, light, life, and fertility to the Incas. Second to Inti in power was the Moon, the Sun's wife. The Earth, the Sea, Venus, and constellations representing animals such as llamas and pumas, were also worshipped. *Illapa*, god of thunder and war, controlled hail and rain. The sharp crack of Illapa's sling as he let loose a thunderbolt, heralded the breaking of a storm.

ORACLES AND PRIESTS

The Incas were a superstitious people who would not do anything important without first asking an oracle or priest to consult the spirits on their behalf. Oracles also foretold the future, predicted the outcome of battles, and studied omens to find out who might be guilty of a crime.

In times of trouble, an oracle might recommend making sacrifices of cloth, miniature figures, or animals. The sacrifice of white llamas was considered especially effective, although a poor person might satisfy the gods with a guinea pig. In dire times, such as when a drought, earthquake, or other disaster occurred, the Incas sacrificed humans.

This is a great temple to the Sun God, built by the Incas. In the background are priests' houses and storehouses. A procession of priests and a sacrificial llama winds its way through the temple. At the top of the page is revealed Coricancha, the magnificent temple in Cuzco.

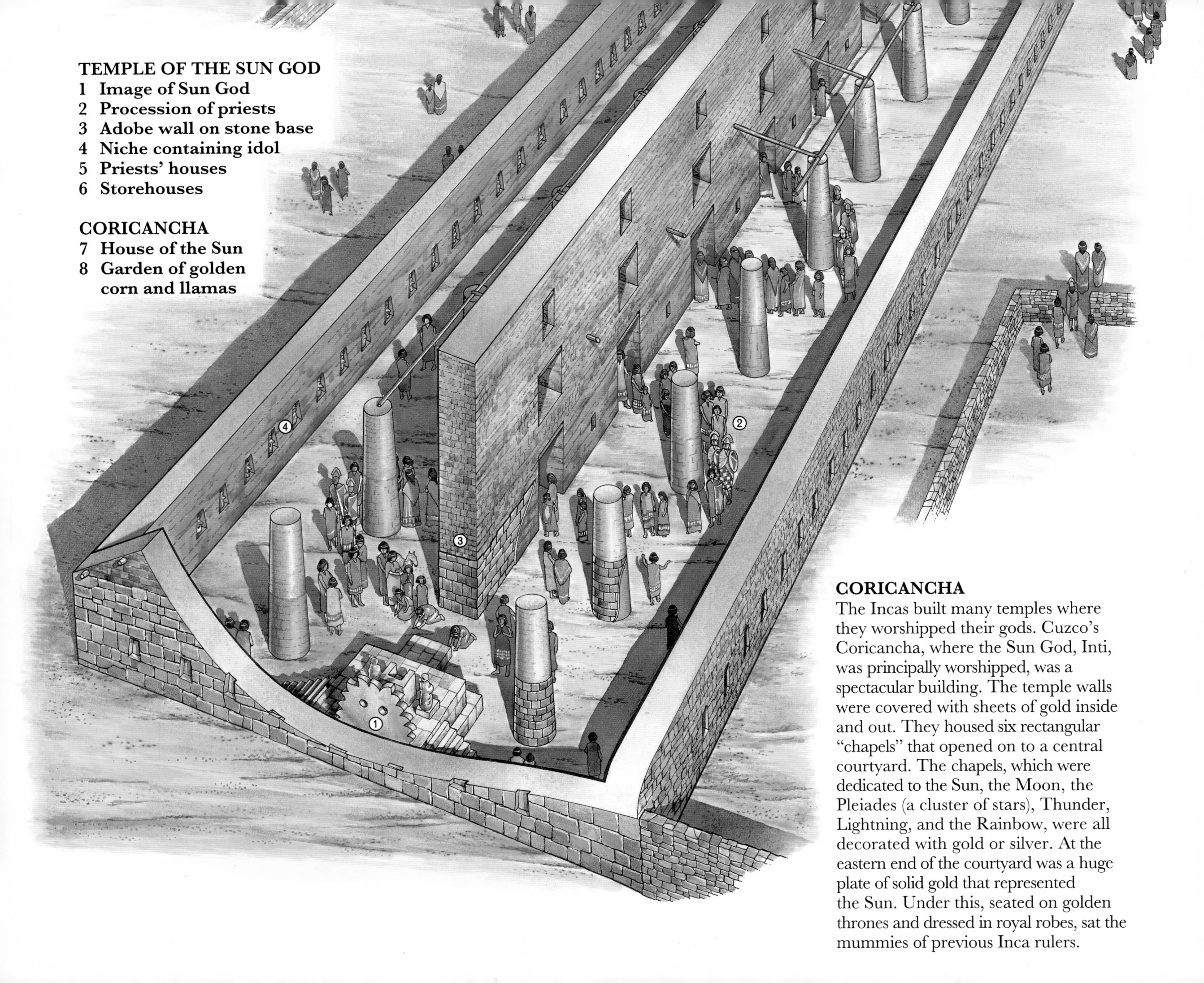

TEMPLE OF THE SUN GOD

1 Image of Sun God
2 Procession of priests
3 Adobe wall on stone base
4 Niche containing idol
5 Priests' houses
6 Storehouses

CORICANCHA

7 House of the Sun
8 Garden of golden
  corn and llamas

CORICANCHA

The Incas built many temples where they worshipped their gods. Cuzco's Coricancha, where the Sun God, Inti, was principally worshipped, was a spectacular building. The temple walls were covered with sheets of gold inside and out. They housed six rectangular "chapels" that opened on to a central courtyard. The chapels, which were dedicated to the Sun, the Moon, the Pleiades (a cluster of stars), Thunder, Lightning, and the Rainbow, were all decorated with gold or silver. At the eastern end of the courtyard was a huge plate of solid gold that represented the Sun. Under this, seated on golden thrones and dressed in royal robes, sat the mummies of previous Inca rulers.

PRIESTS AND DOCTORS

A Chimu gold ceremonial knife with a llama on the handle decorated with turquoise. Knives similar to this were used by Inca priests during religious ceremonies—perhaps even for human sacrifice.

Priests ran the temples and organized the religious ceremonies that were such an important part of the Incas' life. There were so many priests that some historians think there were more of them than soldiers in Peru. More than 4,000 people worked at Coricancha alone as priests or Handmaidens of the Sun, or in humbler roles as shepherds of the Sun God's flocks, porters of his goods, and sweepers of his floors.

THE HIGH PRIEST

The power and importance of any priest depended on the shrine where he worked and the tasks he did there. Sun priests had more prestige and influence than other priests. The most important priest of all was the *vilcaoma*, the High Priest of the Sun, who was always a close relative of the Sapa Inca. He led a very simple life, but he and the priests who assisted him were all nobles. They formed an inner circle that wielded great power and influence at court. Away from Cuzco, the priests who worked in the temples of the Sun and for the great huacas all came from families of the curacas. The least important priests were those appointed by each village to serve their local gods.

A young priestess is taken by priests to be sacrificed to the Sun God. Human sacrifice was only carried out by the Incas in times of dire emergency, such as a long drought or a major earthquake.

34

DOCTORS

Inca priests also acted as doctors. Some of their cures seem more like magic than medicine, and involved charms, trances, chants, and spells. Among the charms the Incas thought most effective were bezoars. These were stones eaten by some animals, such as the tapir, to aid their digestion.

But in some ways Inca doctors were far in advance of European doctors of the times. Inca doctors could cure many serious illnesses including dysentery, ulcers, eye problems, lice, and toothaches. They used a wide variety of herbal medicines which they got from *hampi camayoc*, the keepers of authorized remedies or state chemists. They also got medicines from *collahuaya*, or peddlers, who carried medicinal plants, amulets, and lucky charms. One of the most effective Inca medicines was quinine, which was used to dress wounds and sores and to cure fever.

An Inca worshipping at a huaca. The tower in the background is a chullpa—*a type of burial tower built by the Tiahuanacoans. The Incas learned some of their stoneworking skills from this earlier civilization.*

SURGEON-PRIESTS

Inca priests were also skilled surgeons who could amputate crushed or diseased limbs, and even perform brain surgery. Most villages had a *sancoyoc* or surgeon-priest who could treat broken limbs and open abscesses, or pull out teeth. The most skillful surgeons traveled with the army or treated nobles in the large cities. The surgeon-priests anaesthetized their patients by making them chew coca leaves or drink large amounts of chicha, or by hypnosis. They performed operations using knives made of flint, obsidian, gold, copper, or silver. They knew how to burn wounds to prevent infection. They bit off the heads of large ants and used the jaws as clips to close wounds, just as modern surgeons use stitches.

BLOOD TRANSFUSIONS

We know that surgeon-priests performed blood transfusions about 500 years before the practice became common elsewhere in the world. Because many Incas belonged to the same blood group, bad reactions in a patient were surprisingly rare.

DEATH AND BURIAL

When an Inca died, his or her body might be mummified and treated as a sacred object. Graves were treated with great respect since dead people were believed to protect the living. Members of a dead person's family visited their relative's grave regularly to make offerings, perhaps of flowers or food. Failure to make the necessary offerings and sacrifices invited the wrath of the dead person's spirit. The shrines of the dead were tended by elderly men who were no longer able to do heavy manual work.

An Inca priest performs a magical cure. We now know that the mind can play an important role in illness. Perhaps the treatments performed by Inca doctors were more successful with patients who believed strongly in the power of the Sun God.

An Inca surgeon trepanned, or cut open, this person's skull, perhaps to let out evil spirits, or perhaps to make the skull into a more regular shape. It would be interesting to know how long the patient survived.

The sling was the long-range weapon of choice for the Incas. The sling, shown above with a sling stone, is made entirely of wool. Below it are two club heads made of obsidian.

The Inca army was almost always victorious in battle because it was bigger, could usually move faster, and was better organized than the armies of the tribes against which it fought.

PART-TIME SOLDIERS

The only full-time army in the empire was the Sapa Inca's bodyguard of about 10,000 soldiers. These soldiers were recruited from the nobility. Other soldiers were usually ordinary farmers who might be serving their mit'a. Each province had to supply a certain number of able-bodied men for the army. The actual number depended on the size of the province's population.

ARMOR AND WEAPONS

Soldiers wore quilted cotton protective tunics and wooden or braided cane helmets with wool fringes. Their backs were protected by plates of iron-hard chonta wood. They carried shields made from wood or toughened animal hides.

The Incas usually fought with clubs. These were three-foot wooden shafts tipped with heavy bronze or stone heads shaped like a star. The Incas also fought with spears and with two-handed swords made of chonta wood.

STOREHOUSES

The Inca army was sustained by an excellent supply system. Supplies were kept in the thousands of qollqas scattered throughout the empire. In peacetime they protected the Incas from the worst effects of famine. In wartime they ensured that an army on a campaign was as well fed and equipped as an army resting in Cuzco. Some qollqas were stocked with a huge variety of food including chuño, dried meat, and *cumo* (various preserved foods). Other storehouses were full of cloaks, wool, cloth, and military equipment. Some supplies were carried with the army on llamas. The llamas could also be slaughtered for food.

GOING TO WAR

When war broke out, the qollqas were filled with supplies. Great numbers of warriors were summoned and put into companies according to their ayllus. The army set out along the excellent roads.

In the meantime, ambassadors were sent to the trouble spot. There they made terrible threats, but also promised gifts and honor if the enemy surrendered. If the enemy refused, the Inca army attacked with great violence. There were few battle tactics. The slingers tossed their stones and then the warriors closed in with maces. The battle soon became a chaotic mêlée which the Incas nearly always won by sheer force of numbers.

The Incas used a few simple tactics such as setting fire to the grass to confuse their enemies, and dividing their forces to attack from two sides. But once the two armies joined battle, they just fought fiercely until one side won.

TERRIBLE REVENGE

Defeated enemies were slaughtered and their heads were cut off. Skulls were plated with gold and made into goblets. Enemy teeth were made into necklaces. Captives were paraded through Cuzco and laid in front of the Sun temple while the Sapa Inca trod on their necks as a symbol of victory. Some were skinned and their skins made into gruesome drums in the shape of the human body. When the drum was played the dead soldier appeared to be beating his own belly with drumsticks.

THE INCAS TAKE CONTROL

After conquest, a clay relief model of the conquered area, along with a census of people, animals, and produce, was taken to Cuzco. Local gods, customs, dress, and language were respected but the defeated tribe had to agree to worship the Sun God. Local chieftains were either put to death or sent to Cuzco to learn Quechua and be trained in Inca ways. Ayllus were established along Inca lines. Roads were extended into the conquered area. Architects were sent to build new towns and a temple to the Sun God. If the population was hostile it was resettled to another area, and loyal people called *mitimaes* were moved in to replace them. The area became an Inca province.

Golden skull cups were made from the skulls of the Incas' fiercest enemies. They were carried by the generals as ceremonial objects.

An Inca general is carried to battle on a litter as he whirls his sling round his head. This picture was drawn about 1620, long after the Spanish conquest, so it may not be entirely accurate.

37

There was no form of wheeled transportation in the Inca empire, because the Incas had not invented the wheel. They did not have horses either, so most people had to go by foot. They traveled on the spectacular roads that stretched over 15,000 miles through the Inca lands. This amazing road system was one of the major reasons for the success of the Inca empire.

Inca suspension bridges were made of braided ropes called cabuya *which were plaited and twisted into cables that could be as thick as a human's body. Several cables spanned the river and were anchored by massive stone pillars and heavy stone weights. Wood and bamboo planks laid across the cables formed the floor of the bridge.*

THE IMPORTANCE OF ROADS

Inca roads were the veins and arteries of the empire. The Inca armies marched along them as they moved to repel invading tribes or to conquer new lands. The roads were important supply routes for llama trains carrying goods from one part of the empire to another. They were also a vital communication network along which traveled the messengers and officials who were the eyes, ears, and voice of the Sapa Inca.

FEATS OF ENGINEERING

Many Inca roads crossed high mountains. On steep slopes Inca engineers built stone steps that looked like giant flights of stairs. These steps were no obstacle to travelers on foot or to the sure-footed llamas and guanacos used as pack animals. The Incas also built special jungle roads, wide military roads, gold roads, and royal roads. The Andean royal road, which was over 3,500 miles long, was longer than the longest Roman road. Inca engineers developed special techniques to deal with particular problems. They built low walls alongside roads in desert areas to keep the sand from drifting over the road's surface. In swamps they raised roads on stone causeways.

BRIDGES

Where roads had to cross steep valleys or ravines, Inca engineers built bridges. They used reed boats as pontoons to bridge wide, slow-flowing rivers. These were common around Lake Titicaca where reeds were plentiful. The Incas also built simple cantilever bridges to cross narrow streams. However, their most spectacular bridges were suspension bridges built across deep ravines.

THE ROYAL ROAD

The main Inca highway was known as *Capac-nan*, the "Royal Road." It ran from Cuzco to Quito and was over 1,400 miles long. Built from dovetailed blocks of stone, the road was arrow-straight for most of its length and a uniform 26 feet wide. As with many Inca roads, trees were planted alongside the Royal Road to give travelers shade. A ditch ran parallel to the road, carrying a stream of fresh water so travelers could quench their thirst and water their animals. Every 15 to 30 miles there were *tambos* (rest houses) where messengers and travelers could stay the night.

MARKETS

Many of the people traveling on the Inca roads were traders. However, trade was very limited. Only those goods not set aside for the Sapa Inca or the Sun God could be traded. There was little trade with people outside the empire.

Trade took place at local markets called *catus*. The Incas had no money so they used a barter system to exchange goods. People from the highlands swapped llama wool, chuñu, and *charki* (dried meat) for lowland products such as salt, shells, fish, corn, cotton, fruits, and beans. Jungle people brought feathers, iron-hard palm chonta wood, birds, dyes, rubber, tobacco, and herbal medicines. Everyone traded for manufactured goods such as cloth and pottery. Exchange was busiest in the harvest season.

Teams of workers did labor duty building and repairing the Royal Road. The road passed through steamy swamps, teeming rainforest, icy plateaus, and arid desert. It spanned deep ravines by means of suspension bridges. In some places the road climbed to altitudes of over 16,000 feet.

MESSENGERS

The Sapa Inca kept in touch with all the corners of the empire through a network of messengers. Messages were memorized or recorded on quipus.

MESSENGERS

Inca messengers were known as *chasquis*. They were chosen from the fittest and fastest young men. Four to six chasquis lived in cabins built along the main roads. Two of the chasquis were posted as lookouts—keeping watch in both directions.

RELAYING A MESSAGE

Messengers were easily recognized by the large white-feathered headdresses they wore. As soon as a messenger was spotted in the distance, one of the chasquis would race to meet him. The chasquis ran beside the incoming messenger, listening while the message was repeated to him. If the messenger carried a quipu, the chasquis would take it from him.

Once he was sure he had the message perfectly memorized, the chasquis ran on toward the next relay station leaving the tired messenger behind to rest in the cabin. In this way messages could travel over 250 miles in a single day.

EMERGENCY MESSAGES

If a message brought news of an emergency, such as an invasion or a rebellion, a warning signal could be sent by a chain of bonfires. As each group of chasquis saw smoke or flames rising from the next relay station, they lit a bonfire of their own. In this way news of the peril reached Cuzco more rapidly than the fastest runner. The Sapa Inca could order his army to set out at once, marching toward the bonfires before the actual cause of the alarm was known. The general marching with the army would eventually meet one of the messengers on the route and learn from him the exact nature of the emergency.

1 **Hall where travelers, messengers, and soldiers could stay**
2 **Soldiers erecting a tent**
3 **Small temple**
4 **Royal or official's apartment**
5 **Sunken bath**
6 **Signal fire**
7 **Llama pen**

INCA WAY STATIONS

Some of the tambos built at intervals along the roads were probably little more than simple cabins where tired messengers could rest. Others seem to have been much more elaborate centers.

On the larger sites, archaeological excavations have revealed remains of what were probably halls used for official and military business and as a place for travelers to stay, royal apartments where the Sapa Inca and his family would rest, and a temple where travelers could worship the Sun God. The remains of storehouses and baths have also been found.

The see-through scene below shows a way station, with a unit of the Inca army arriving. A few of the soldiers will be able to stay in the long hall on the right. The rest of the patrol will have to sleep in the open. We know the Inca soldiers used tents. When the see-through page is turned, you can see inside the hall as well as the apartments and offices in the compound on the left. A soldier is pointing at smoke rising from behind the hills—is this a warning of an enemy army?

41

THE SPANISH ARRIVE

Francisco Pizarro, the conqueror of Peru. He was about 57 years old in 1532 and could neither read nor write. He was drawn to Tumbes by rumors that a rich empire lay somewhere to the south. After his soldiers had destroyed the Inca empire, he was savagely criticized.

In 1532, a small Spanish ship sailed into the Inca port of Tumbes. It carried 110 foot soldiers, 67 cavalry, and one small cannon. This tiny force was led by adventurer Francisco Pizarro. He had been appointed by King Charles V of Spain to be the new governor of Peru. South America was a continent that the Spanish had only just discovered. Pizarro wanted gold and power and he planned to get them by any means. Within a few weeks Pizarro's small body of men had brought the mighty Inca empire to its knees.

DIVISION OF THE EMPIRE

In 1493, when Huayna Capac became Sapa Inca, the empire had reached its greatest power. In 1527, Huayna became very ill, probably from smallpox, a devastating disease brought by Europeans to the New World. The Incas had no immunity against European diseases, and it is estimated that as many as 250,000 Incas may have died of smallpox before any of them even saw a European. Huayna died without naming his successor. Many people thought Huáscar, son of Huayna and his coya, should be the new Sapa Inca. Others, including many Inca generals, preferred Huayna's elder son, Atahualpa, whose mother was not the coya.

CIVIL WAR

Atahualpa decided to challenge his brother for the throne. This decision led to a bitter civil war that Atahualpa finally won. During the ferocious war, thousands of Incas were reported slaughtered. It was rumored that Atahualpa ordered the murder of his brother's entire ayllu. Over 200 of Huayna's sons were killed; some were hung, others were weighted with heavy stones and thrown into rivers or lakes, or hurled off cliffs. All Huáscar's female relatives were hung in trees, some by their hair, some by their arms. There was talk that 1,000 enemy warriors had their hearts torn out and scattered on the battlefields.

How many of these deaths actually happened is hard to say. The Spanish who reported them became the enemies of Atahualpa, and they might have wanted to exaggerate his crimes to excuse their own terrible deeds.

Pizarro's force landed safely then advanced rapidly inland. Pizarro wanted to impress the Incas with his power. He won several battles and burned those chiefs who opposed him. In this way he quickly subdued the northern part of the empire.

EVENTS AT CAJAMARCA

In November 1532, after winning a great victory and capturing his brother, the triumphant Atahualpa went to a town called Cajarmarca. There, in a camp outside the town, surrounded by 50,000 soldiers fresh from their victory against the forces of Huáscar, Atahualpa rested and bathed in the hot springs.

Atahualpa was intrigued to hear that the Spanish strangers were not far away. Atahualpa was curious about these strangers, but not in the least afraid of them. Meanwhile, Pizarro had moved his small force into the town. He sent a message to Atahualpa requesting to meet him the next day. The Sapa Inca, carried on his golden litter, arrived with 6,000 unarmed attendants.

AMBUSH

Atahualpa did not realize that Pizarro had prepared an ambush. The Spanish soldiers hid and waited until the Sapa Inca arrived at the main square. A Spanish priest traveling with Pizarro began to preach to Atahualpa. The Sapa Inca took the priest's Bible and examined it. Never having seen a book before, Atahualpa threw it to the ground in disgust. Almost at once, Pizarro gave the signal to attack. The cannon roared, the musketeers opened fire, and the cavalry charged the Sapa Inca's litter. The Spaniards cut the royal bodyguard down with steel weapons as they tried to defend their lord with their bare hands. Legend says that Pizarro himself seized Atahualpa and took him prisoner.

Atahualpa's bodyguard were unarmed. They were not expecting an ambush and were cut down before they could organize any resistance. Once Atahualpa was a prisoner, the Incas allowed the Spaniards to loot their camp and did not try to rescue their emperor.

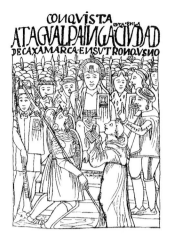

Poma de Ayala's 17th century drawing depicts Atahualpa being shown the Bible by a priest who had traveled with Pizarro's force.

CONQUEST OF THE EMPIRE

By a strange twist of fate, Pizarro had arrived at a time when the Inca empire was divided and weak. By seizing the Sapa Inca, Pizarro cut off the head of power. The Incas, used to obeying orders, did not know what to do and so they did nothing.

A ROOM FULL OF GOLD
Atahualpa realized that the Spaniards desired gold above everything else. He offered to fill a large room with gold piled as high as he could reach if they would set him free. Pizarro asked that a smaller room also be filled twice over with silver. Atahualpa ordered Coricancha to be stripped. The ransom arrived in 200 loads. In one load alone were 700 plates taken from the walls of the temple. Each weighed 5 pounds. This single consignment would be worth millions of dollars today.

After the defeat of the empire, many Incas became slaves working on coca plantations or in mines, such as the huge workings at Potosi where the Spanish found a whole mountain made of silver ore.

An item of booty seized by the conquistadors. This model of an alpaca is made of silver. Many other fine examples of Inca workmanship were stolen and melted down by the Spaniards.

A FANTASTIC TREASURE
After five months, Pizarro decided to divide the gold even though the room had not been filled. The first load was intended for the King of Spain. It consisted of some of the finest examples of Inca craftwork. There were goblets, plates, ornaments, and vases from temples and royal palaces, and imitations of animals and plants, including golden ears of corn with silver leaves. There was so much treasure that some Spaniards replaced their worn out horseshoes with silver ones! This first shipment of treasure disappeared on its way to Spain, and was never seen again.

DIVIDING THE TREASURE

The rest of the treasure was split among Pizarro's band. Each soldier took more than his own weight in gold and silver. Pizarro took many times that, including the Sapa Inca's throne made of solid gold. Pizarro's men, increasingly fearing an Inca attack, began to sleep in full armor. Few of the soldiers would live to spend their wealth.

DEATH OF THE INCA

Once he had his gold, Pizarro decided to do away with Atahualpa. He set up a court of Inquisition (a court where religious "crimes" were tried). Atahualpa was accused of murdering his brother, Huáscar, of having many wives, and of worshipping idols. Atahualpa was found guilty and sentenced to be burned to death. Appalled because destruction of his body would mean he could not live eternally, Atahualpa agreed to convert to Christianity in return for being garrotted (strangled). The sentence was carried out, but in a final betrayal the body of the Sapa Inca was burned and buried.

Pizarro's actions were criticized by many people in Europe. This cartoon shows him greedily considering the profits of his silver mines.

AFTERMATH

Pizarro then led his soldiers to Cuzco. With no regard to how the Incas would feed themselves, the Spaniards stripped the qollqas bare. They treated the Incas cruelly and put a puppet ruler, Manco Capac, on the throne. Inca resistance increased and armed attacks began under Manco. Then the Spanish fell into dissention, quarrelling over who should rule what. Eventually some discontented Spaniards plotted against Pizarro and assassinated him on June 26, 1541.

SPANISH RULE

Over the next few years, the Spanish tried to stamp out the old Inca ways. Sun temples were torn down and replaced with Christian churches. Christian missionaries arrived from Spain to convert the Incas to Christianity. Defeated in battle and ravaged by European diseases, the Incas bowed to the inevitable and came forward to be baptized. Many Incas became slave laborers working in the fields and gold mines of their new rulers. Gradually, many aspects of the Inca culture disappeared. In spite of this, some of the old Inca gods and traditions have survived and are now part of a new and vibrant Andean culture.

A figurine of a mamacona. She is wearing a piece of cloth with typical Inca patterns on it, colored with vegetable and mineral dyes. Items like these were often put into tombs, and so a few survived the Spanish conquest.

This 16th century Inca beaker is made of wood and decorated with painted scenes showing Spaniards. It may, therefore, have been made shortly after the Spanish invasion.

KEY DATES AND GLOSSARY

We know relatively little about the early history of the Incas. The Incas did not keep written records as we know them, and most of their quipus have been destroyed. For this reason the dates given before 1438 can only be approximate.

ca. 3000 B.C. The coast of Peru is occupied by villagers who live by growing crops and fishing.

ca. 1200 B.C. Pottery appears.

ca. 800 B.C. Corn introduced.

ca. A.D. 1200 Start of Inca civilization, and the reigns of the semi-legendary Incas: Manco Capac, Sinchi Roca, Lloque Yupanqui, Mayta Capac, Capac Yupanqui, Inca Roca, Yahuar Huaca, Viracocha, Pachacuti (1438–1471), Topa Inca Yupanqui (1471–1493), and Huayna Capac (1493–1527).

1527 Pizarro lands at Tumbes and discovers the Inca empire. Civil war between Inca Huascar and his half-brother Atahualpa (1528–1532).

1532 Pizarro attacks Atahualpa at Cajamarca. Atahualpa is taken prisoner and held as ransom for a room full of gold.

1533 Atahualpa is executed.

The city of Machu Picchu (below) was built high in the mountains about 50 miles to the northwest of Cuzco. The Spaniards never found the city, whose ruins were discovered in 1911 by an expedition led by Hiram Bingham.

1535 Incas conquered by Spaniards. Manco Capac made Sapa Inca by the Spaniards. Pizarro founds city of Lima.

1537 Manco Capac escapes to Vilcapampa. He leads an attack on Cuzco but fails to capture the city. When Manco Capac is killed by Spanish allies, Sayri Tapac, his son, becomes the new Sapa Inca.

1538 Pizarro executes his partner Diego de Almagro after bitter quarrels.

1541 Pizarro killed by followers of Almagro's son.

1560 Sayri Tapac dies of poison. His brother Titu Cusi proclaims himself Sapa Inca and begins a guerilla war against the Spaniards. He dies of a mysterious disease.

1572 Titu Cusi's brother Tupac Amaru becomes Sapa Inca. He is captured by the Spaniards and executed. This marks the end of the Inca empire.

1580 In the 50 years after the conquest, about 6,000,000 former Inca subjects die, mostly of diseases like smallpox brought from Europe by the Spanish invaders.

1780 A *mestizo* (person of mixed Inca and Spanish blood) calling himself Tupac Amaru after one of the last Inca leaders raises an unsuccessful revolt of Indians and mestizos against Spanish rule. He is executed in 1781.

Glossary

acllacuna: literally, Chosen Women who served the Sapa Inca and the Sun God.

a'ka: a mild alcoholic, malty drink.

ayllu: an Inca clan or social group.

caramayoc: a village headman.

catus: Inca markets.

chasquis: Inca messengers.

chicha: corn beer used in religious ceremonies.

coca: a plant which contains several powerful drugs including cocaine.

coya: the Inca Queen, who was also the sister of the Sapa Inca.

curacas: nobles who were not Incas by blood.

huacas: holy objects or sacred places.

Inti: the Sun God, the most important god.

lampa: an Inca hoe.

locro: an Inca stew made from dried meat and freeze-dried potatoes.

mit'a: a compulsory duty to serve in the army or to help build public works.

mitimaes: settlers sent to newly conquered regions to replace the rebellious population.

mote: corn cooked with peppers and herbs.

orejone: an Inca priest.

qollqa: a state-controlled storehouse.

quipu: literally a "knot," the word was used to describe bundles of knotted cords that the Incas used to keep records.

quipu camayoc: a person whose job it was to remember what the knots on each quipu stood for.

quirau: a cradle for a baby.

runaquipa: an official government counter, so named because of the quipu he used to record the count.

sancoyoc: a priest who was also a doctor.

Sapa Inca: the emperor of the Incas. Literally, the "Unique Inca."

sierra: a mountain range.

taclla: an Inca foot-plow.

Tahuantinsuyu: Land of the Four Quarters, i.e. the Inca empire. Each quarter was one large province ruled by an official called an *apo* who was always a close relative of the Sapa Inca.

tambos: way stations, or rest houses, built on Inca roads.

topo: a plot of land given to a man and his wife upon marriage.

tupu: a gold, silver, or bronze pin used to fasten a cloak.

Quotations

Most of the quotations come from letters and memoirs written by Spanish friars working in Peru after the fall of the Inca empire. Many of them learned to speak Quechua, and they wrote down what they could of Inca history and customs. The line drawings were done by Poma de Ayala, a mestizo, in the early 17th century.

INDEX

Page numbers in italics refer to captions.

Adobe bricks 19, 24, *33*
Amazon rainforests 4, 7
Andean people *4*, 5
Andes mountains 4, *5*
army 6, 9, 35, 36–37, *41*
Atahualpa, Inca 29, 42–43, *43*, 44–45, 46
ayllu (clan) 8–9, 14, 23, *24*, 26, *26*, 31, 32, 37, 42, 47

Babies 30, *31*, 47
battles 37, *37*
Bingham, Hiram *46*
blood transfusions 35
boats *17*, 21
bridges *17*, 38, *38*, *39*
building *18*, 19

Calendar 7
canals 18–19, 39
censuses *13*, 37
ceremonies 11, 23, 30, 31, 34, *34*
Chan Chan 5, *5*
chasquis (messengers) 40, 41, 47
chicha beer *12*, 23, 35, 47
children 30–31, *30*
Chimu people *4*, 5, 7, *34*
Chosen Women 10, 14, 16, *16–17*, 17, 22
Christianity 43
clothes 10, 22, 23–29, *28*, *29*, 31
Coba, Padre 21
Cobo, Bernabé 11
coca plant 21, 35, *44*, 47
communication system 38, 40–41
conquistadors *4*, 29, *44*
Coricancha *32–33*, 33
corn 17, *17*, 20, 21, 32, 46, 47
cotton 26, 28
cradles (*quirau*) 30, *30*, 47
craftwork 26–27
curacas nobles *12*, 13, 14, 22, 34, 47
Cuzco 6–7, 8, 14–15, *14*, *15*, *17*, 31, 32–33, *32–33*, 45

De Ayala, Poma *6*, 23, *43*, 47
de la Vega, Garcilaso 30
death 11, 35
division of labor 9, *9*

doctors 34–35, *35*, 47
dyes 26, *45*

Ear lobe decoration *28*, 29
engineering 18–19, 38
execution 13, *13*

Farming 8, *8*, 15, 18, *20*, 20–21, 47
featherwork *26*, 27, 29, *29*
festivals *10*, 14, *28*
fishing *21*, 36
food 20–21, 23
fortress 15, *15*
freeze-drying 20, 47

Garcilaso, Inca 17
gods 17, 32
gold, booty 44–45, *44*; craft 4, *4*, 5, 7, *11*, 27, 33, *34*, 37, *37*
government 8, 12–13
grinding corn 23, 25, *25*
guano fertilizer 19

Helmet *9*, 24, 36
houses 24–25, *24–25*
huaca 32, 34, 35, 47
Huáscar, Inca 42, 43, 46
Huayna Capac 42, 46

Lake Titicaca 5, *5*, 16–17, *16–17*
laws 7, 12–13, *12*
llamas 21, 24, 26, *27*, 36, 38, *41*

Machu Picchu 19, 25, *46*
mamacona 22, 45
market 39, 47
marriage 22, 31
messengers 40, 47
mit'a 9, *9*, 39, 47
Moon God 17
mummies 5, *19*, 11, 33, *35*

Observatory 15, *15*

Pachacuti Inca Yupanqui 6–7, *6*, 12, 14, 32, 46
panaca 11, 47
Pizarro, Francisco 42–43, *42*, 44–45, *45*, 46
potatoes 4, 20, 47
pottery 5, *12*, *21*, *26*, 27, 31, 46
priestesses 22, 23, *23*, *34*

priests 15, 32, 34–35, *34–35*, 47
punishments 13, *13*

Qollqas 9, 20, 26, 36–37, 41, 43, 45, 47
Quecha 6, 14, 37
quipu 11, *12*, *13*, 27, 40, 46, 47

Rememberers 11, 47
road system 6, 37, 38–39, *39*

Sacrifice 23, 31, 32, *32–33*, 34
Sacsahuamán 14–15. *15*, *29*
Sapa Inca 8, 10–11, *10*, 12–13, 16, 47; *coya* 23, *23*, 42, 47; wives 23, *23*
signal fires 41, *41*
silverwork 27, *27*
skull cups 37, *37*
slaves *44*, 45
slings *36*, 37
smallpox 42, 46
South American people 4–5, *5*
Spanish conquest 37, 42–45, *43*
spinning 23, 26
stone building *18*, 19, 25, 35
Sun God (Inti) 8, 10, *11*, 22, 23, 32, 34, *34*, 37, 47; temples 14, *23*, 32–33, *32–33*

Tahuantinsuyu 12, 47
taxes 8–9
temples 17, 34, 41
tents *40–41*
terracing 4, 5, 17, 18–19
throne 10, *10*, 15, 43
Tiahuanaco 5, *5*, 35
tools 18, 19
Topa Inca Yupanqui 7, 46
topo (land) 8, 47
totem 9, 24
trade 39
travel 38–39
tunics 28, 36, 47
tupu (pin) 28, *29*, 47

Uru tribe 16, *16*, 17

Warriors *5*, 24, 31, 37
way stations (*tambos*) 39, 40–41, *40–41*, 47
weapons 36
weaving 22, 26, 27
women 22–23, *23*
wool 10, 22, 26, *27*, 28, 29